Nibheis Beinn 's Gleann   **Nevis** The Ben and the Glen

First published in 2010 by The Nevis Partnership
Unit 6 & 7, Lochaber Rural Complex,
Torlundy, Fort William PH33 6SW
email: info@nevispartnership.co.uk
tel: 01397 701901

www.nevispartnership.co.uk

All maps © **Harvey Maps**
12-22 Main Street, Doune FK16 6BJ

A CIP catalogue record for this book is
available from the British Library
Further copies of this publication available
from the publishers address above.

ISBN: 978-0-9565817-0-9

design and production: **Hillside Agency**
original concept: **Anna Trafford**

Com-pairteachas Nibheis
The Nevis Partnership

photography

front cover: **D. Barnes/ScottishViewpoint.com**
title page: **Alex Gillespie**
contents: top **Alan Kimber**, bottom - **Alex Gillespie**
back cover: left - **Forestry Commission Picture Library/Isobel Cameron**; right – **Alex Gillespie**

Images are reproduced courtesy of:
Alan Kimber: page 28 main pic, page 30 main pic, page 33 top
Alastair Cumming: page 30 top left
Alex Gillespie: pages 9, 10 bottom, 13, 14 bottom, 17, 20 bottom right, 22, 24, 25 top, 27, 28 top right, 30 top right, 31, 32 top right & bottom right, 34, 37 top middle & centre right, 38, page 40 top centre & right, middle left & right, 42 middle top & bottom & top right, 43 bottom left and right, 44 & 45, 46 top and bottom left.
Anna Trafford: page 20 bottom left, 33 bottom
www.blazin-fiddles.co.uk: page 21
Brian Wilshaw: page 14 top, 28 top middle left, 42 left, 43 top left
Bridget Thomas: page 32 top left & bottom left
Dan Bailey: page 42 bottom right
Forestry Commission Picture Library/Isobel Cameron:
page 26, page 28 top centre right, page 32 bottom centre left, page 37 bottom left
Highland Council and **www.ambaile.org.uk**:
page 19 top from James Logan's The Clans of the Scottish Highlands publ. 1845, bottom from W Drummond Norie's Loyal Lochaber. Historical Genealogical and Traditionary publ. 1898
Highland Council Ranger Service/Fiona McLean: page 14 middle
Ian Abernethy: page 16 , 18 middle & bottom,
Ian Strachan: page 37 top left & top right & middle left & centre, bottom middle, 40 top left & centre middle & bottom left & middle & right,
Kathleen MacPherson/Lochaber Archive Centre: page 18 top
Lochaber Geopark/Alex Gillespie: page 8 bottom
Lorne Gill/Scottish Natural Heritage:
page 36 bottom right & bottom left, 37 bottom right, 41
Mike Pescod: page 28 top left, 30 middle left
National Library of Scotland (with kind permission of the Trustees of): page 20 - top from Ordnance Survey 1: 2,500 Inverness-shire Mainland Sheet CL8 publ. 1876
Noel Williams: page 8 top, 10 top, 11, 12
Oban Times: page 23
Rio Tinto Alcan: page 25 bottom

Nibheis Beinn 's Gleann

Nevis The Ben and the Glen

Written and edited by
Kate McKinley

Nibheis Beinn 's Gleann

Nevis The Ben and the Glen

An extraordinary mountain and a beautiful glen

This book is compiled by
The Nevis Partnership

The Nevis Partnership helps
protect, manage and enhance the
Nevis area so visitors can continue
to enjoy this unique landscape
both now and in the future.

www.nevispartnership.co.uk

opposite
Top: The craggy north face of Ben
Nevis is a mecca for winter climbing.
Bottom: Glen Nevis is a classic
glacial 'U' shaped valley.

TOWERING ABOVE the rest of Britain,
Ben Nevis draws people like a giant magnet.

Each year all kinds of people - mountaineers, climbers, runners and visitors enjoying a break in one of the most magical areas of Scotland - slog their way up 1344m for the sheer thrill of standing on the summit of the highest mountain in the United Kingdom.

This book is all about this extraordinary mountain and the beautiful glen which runs along its base.

It's designed to guide you through one of the most iconic living landscapes in the British Isles - a place rich in cultural, social and natural history.

It's an incredibly diverse area too. You can be on an arctic plateau and then back at sea level all in just a single day.

This is also an ancient place, where the rocks, hills, corries and valleys you see today first started to take shape millions of years ago.

No wonder the Ben and the Glen – as they are affectionately called by the people who live here – attract tens of thousands of visitors from all over the world every year.

This book brings the stories of this outstanding area of Scotland to life. It's packed with illustrations and photographs of the land and the people who have lived here and those who continue to make this magnificent area their home.

Each chapter also gives fascinating insights and facts on the mountain, the glen and some of the things you might encounter during your visit.

So whether you're on foot, bike, kayak or car, take this book with you. It could just be one of the best travelling companions you've had.

Ben Nevis and Glen Nevis are justifiably popular and every year tens of thousands of people are blessed by this particular mountain and its scenic glen. While we Scots enjoy the best access arrangements in the world, that freedom to climb the mountain and roam in the glen brings with it responsibilities. In short the Nevis area needs all the help it can get, from people like you. Can you put something back? Can you give a little time, or money, to help Ben Nevis and Glen Nevis maintain their iconic status? If you can, that would be absolutely tremendous. Let's all remember the words of the great John Muir and 'Do something for wildness, and make the mountains glad.' Thank you.

Cameron McNeish
Chairman, The Nevis Partnership

To find out how to help or donate, go to:
www.friendsofnevis.co.uk

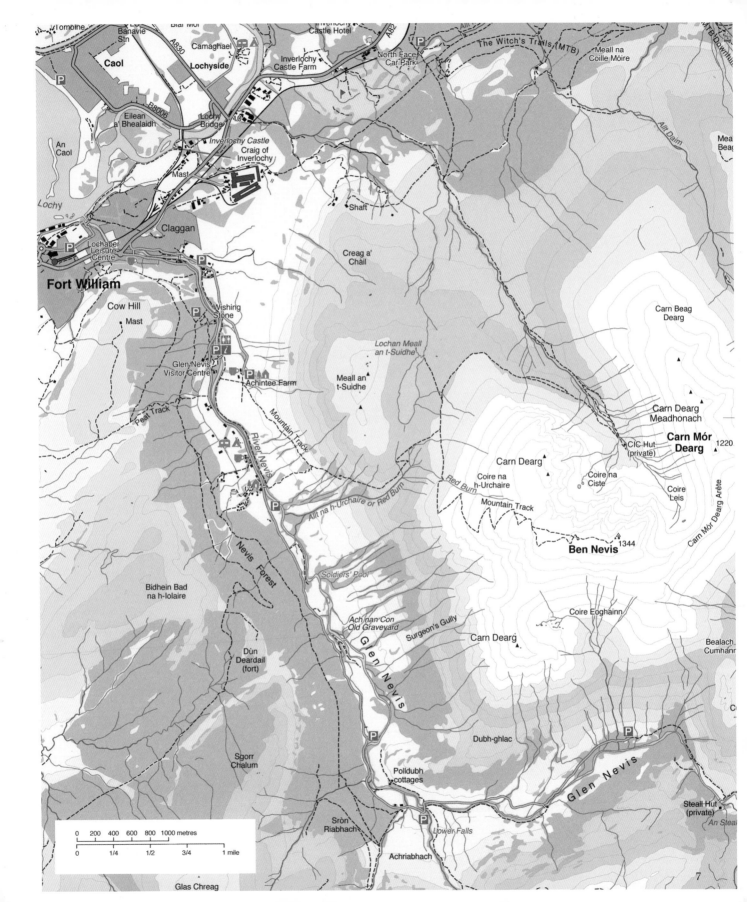

Tomoine
Banavie
Stn
Camaghael
Caol
Lochyside
Blar Mòr
Inverlochy Castle Hotel
A82
North Face Car Park
The Witch's Trails (MTB)
Meall na Coille Mòire
MTB Downhill

Eilean a' Bhealaidh
B8006
Lochy Bridge
10
Inverlochy Castle Farm
Allt Dàim
Meall Beag

An Caol
Inverlochy Castle
Craig of Inverlochy
Shaft
Lochy
Mast

Claggan
Creag a' Chàil
Carn Beag Dearg

Fort William
Lochaber Leisure Centre
Cow Hill
Mast
Wishing Stone
Glen Nevis Visitor Centre
Achintee Farm
Lochan Meall an t-Suidhe
Meall an t-Suidhe
Carn Dearg Meadhonach
Carn Mór Dearg
1220
CIC Hut (private)

Peat Track
River Nevis
Mountain Track
Allt na h-Urchaire or Red Burn
Red Burn
Carn Dearg
Coire na h-Urchaire
Mountain Track
Coire na Ciste
Coire Leis
Carn Mór Dearg Arête

Nevis Forest
Soldiers' Pool
1344
Ben Nevis

Bidhein Bad na h-Iolaire
Ach nan Con Old Graveyard
Surgeon's Gully
Carn Dearg
Coire Eoghainn

Dùn Deardail (fort)
Glen Nevis
Dubh-ghlac
Bealach Cumhann

Sgorr Chalum
Polldubh cottages
Glen Nevis
Steall Hut (private)
An Steall

Sròn Riabhach
Lower Falls
Achriabhach

Glas Chreag

0 200 400 600 800 1000 metres
0   1/4   1/2   3/4   1 mile

7

above
The U-shaped profile of lower Glen Nevis indicates it was once filled by a glacier

The original position of the rocks before the collapse of the Ben Nevis caldera

600m (2000ft)

Chapter 1

Geology: the story behind the scenery in Glen Nevis

Geòlas

GLEN NEVIS IS widely recognised as one of the most beautiful and spectacular glens in Scotland. It is bordered by more than twenty different mountain peaks including mighty Ben Nevis – Britain's highest mountain.

But how did this extraordinary place come into being? What shaped and formed the glen and mountains we see today?

The story behind the scenery is as dramatic and exciting as the landscape itself. It is a story of mountain building, fire and ice.

As you make your way up the glen you'll notice a number of quite obvious changes to the landscape as you leave the busy lower reaches and follow the River Nevis upstream for some 18km to its desolate watershed at Tom an Eite.

The lower part of the glen has steep sides and a relatively flat floor. This distinctive U-shaped profile is a common feature seen in alpine regions and tells us that not all that long ago this glen was filled by a huge glacier.

In the second part of the glen above the Lower Falls, there are many crags and rock outcrops, which show evidence of having been smoothed and scraped by ice.

Mountain Building

While it is relatively easy to imagine that ice played a big part in the shaping of Glen Nevis, the story revealed by the rocks themselves is even more astonishing. Most of the rocks seen in the glen were originally laid down as sediments on the sea floor some 700 million years ago. Layers of quartz, sand and mud were buried and turned into sandstone and siltstone.

Then, at a later date, these rocks were squeezed and crumpled on a huge scale. This squeezing came about when two great 'plates' collided with each other some 450 million years ago. This massive squeeze resulted in the formation of the Caledonian Mountain chain with huge peaks up to 6000m high. The original sedimentary rocks – sandstone and siltstone - were changed by heat and pressure and turned into metamorphic rocks - quartzite and schist.

One of the most remarkable features of the rocks forming the Mamores on the south side of Glen Nevis is that they have been turned completely upside down. Normally younger rocks are found on top of older ones, but in the Mamores the exact opposite is the case.

The route through the dramatic Nevis Gorge to view An Steall – commonly called Steall Waterfall - is one of the most popular walks in the area. If you look carefully where the water spills down the hillside, you can make out the layers or strata in the white quartzite rock dipping from left to right across the falls.

The same quartzite rock layers seen here near the floor of the glen are folded completely back on themselves to form the conspicuous white summits of two nearby mountains –Sgurr a' Mhaim and Stob Ban - both of which are around 1000m high. The quartzite on these two summits is sometimes mistaken for snow in summertime. It's amazing to realise that the schist forming the crags in the lower part of the glen was once on top of these rocks.

Steall Falls and Nevis Gorge

1. Around 410 million years ago a volcano erupts onto a land surface of metamorphic rocks (eroded Caledonian mountains). Initial deposits, which include volcanic breccia, are covered by numerous andesite lava flows.

2. The lavas fill in a depression in the landscape. Some of the ash falls settle into freshwater lochans.

3. A large body of magma rises within the crust.

4. The magma cools and crystallises to form the OUTER GRANITE. The area is then subjected to sideways tension. Vertical fractures develop in the crust and molten material is erupted to the surface along these fissures to create dykes.

5. The dykes cool and crystallise. Some time later a new body of magma rises within the crust.

6. Pressure from the new magma domes up the roof of the magma chamber. When the magma subsides slightly the roof can no longer support itself and a cylindrical fracture develops.

7. When the fracture is complete the roof starts to fail. (The wavy black lines mark the present day land surface.)

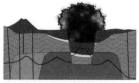

8. A cylindrical block starts to sink down into the magma chamber. Vast quantities of gas and hot ash escape around the margins of the sinking block.

9. A CALDERA is formed at the surface and fresh lavas are erupted into this giant crater.

10. Eventually volcanic activity ceases. The magma then cools and crystallises to form the INNER GRANITE.

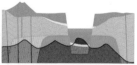

11. Over the next 100 million years huge quantities of rock are removed by erosion. In the succeeding 250 million years large parts of the Highlands are at times submerged by the sea.

12. Renewed uplift of the Scottish Highlands began some 50 million years ago. Repeated glaciations over the last 2 million years have shaped the landscape we see today.

 VOLCANIC BRECCIA

 OUTER GRANITE

 INNER GRANITE

 SCHIST and other metamorphic rocks

 ANDESITE LAVA

 DYKE

Did you know:

Most people climbing Ben Nevis today find the 1344m pull from sea level to the summit challenge enough. They will probably be relieved to learn that, but for the extraordinary events of 410 million years ago, they would have had to carry on for a further 600m!

Fire

Soon after the Caledonian Mountains had been uplifted, huge quantities of magma formed within the Earth's crust. Some of this magma escaped to the surface and poured out as lava. Remains of these lavas can be seen forming the upper half of Ben Nevis. The large rock fragments which cover the ground on the upper part of the mountain are all made of these grey volcanic lavas.

Two huge magma chambers developed in the Glen Nevis area. One formed in the Mamores and another formed directly beneath what is now the summit of Ben Nevis.

Eventually the roof above the Ben Nevis magma chamber could no longer support itself. In a cataclysmic event, which would have blasted vast quantities of ash into the atmosphere, a great mass of crust collapsed 600m into the magma chamber and a huge circular crater called a caldera was formed.

The remaining magma eventually cooled slowly within the crust to form large bodies of granite. Mullach nan Coirean in the Mamores is an obvious red colour because of the granite it is formed from. The Ben Nevis granite can be seen forming the spectacular waterslide immediately above the top car park in Glen Nevis. It also forms the neighbouring mountains of Carn Mor Dearg and Aonach Mor.

The heat which spread out from these magma chambers caused new minerals to develop in the neighbouring rocks. This is why the schist that forms the crags at Polldubh is especially sound and rough.

Schist is not normally a good rock for climbing on as it tends to be is slippery and friable. However, the extra 'baking' given to the schist in Glen Nevis is the reason why it has become a very popular location for rock climbers.

There are also some outcrops of impure limestone in places in the glen. This rock

above left:
The creation of Ben Nevis

is of especial interest to botanists because of the varied flora it attracts. There is a band cutting through Meall Cumhann, the hill overlooking the Nevis Gorge. The rock is normally grey in colour, but in Glen Nevis it shows conspicuous green and cream banding because of the extra heating it received from the Ben Nevis magma.

After all this dramatic volcanic activity there is a 400million year gap in the story recorded in Glen Nevis.

During that time the continental crust which included 'Scotland ' gradually migrated northwards from the southern hemisphere. It crossed the equator some 300 million years ago, by which time many millions of years of erosion had largely worn down the original Caledonian Mountains.

The rocks we see today represent the 'roots' of that ancient mountain chain. It is estimated that the rocks in Glen Nevis were at one time buried some 20km below the surface, so enormous amounts of material must have disappeared to reveal the rocks we see today.

Around 60 million years ago there was another great outburst of igneous activity, this time down the west coast of Scotland as Greenland started to separate from Europe. This eventually led to the opening of the North Atlantic Ocean. Most of the evidence for this event is found further west in the Hebrides where large quantities of lava and other igneous rocks can be seen on islands such as Mull, Rum and Skye.

However, those making an ascent of the mountain track up Ben Nevis should keep their eyes peeled for a feature linked to these events.

At a height of about 350m, between the two aluminium bridges, there is a distinctive band of dark-coloured rock running parallel to the path. The rock breaks apart into spherical layers – also called 'onion-skin weathering'. This band of rock is a feature called a dyke. It was created when lava erupted from a narrow vertical fissure. This particular dyke, because of its orientation is thought to originate from the Skye volcanic centre around 60 million years ago.

Ice

The Earth's climate has fluctuated in dramatic fashion over the last two million years, varying from very cold glacial episodes to much milder interglacials. The final sculpting of the glen was brought about by flowing ice during these multiple glaciations.

At times the ice was extremely thick and even Ben Nevis was completely covered in ice. At its maximum extent a great ice sheet extended as far south as London and the Thames Valley. At other times the ice build up was more limited and the major mountain summits remained uncovered. It was during the most recent glacial episode around 12,000 years ago that most of the upper part of Ben Nevis remained free of ice.

However, regular freeze-thaw action caused the surface rocks to split apart into numerous fragments, known as blockfield. This is a very obvious feature on the upper section of the mountain.

The glen remains a superb area for studying glacial features. As well as the classic U-shaped profile, there are numerous corries, arêtes (thin, almost knife-like ridges of rock) and hanging valleys.

Halfway between the Lower Falls and the top car park beside some Scots Pines there is also a fine example of a roche mountonnée. This whale-backed rock outcrop has a steep and irregular downstream face and a more gentle, smoothed upstream flank. It shows clear evidence of having been shaped and scraped by ice flowing down the glen.

Once the last ice had melted away, the valley sides were no longer supported by ice. Some sections of hillside subsequently became unstable and large rock slope failures have taken place in several places, notably in the middle and upper glen.

So there's more than meets the eye in Glen Nevis. Mountain building, fire and ice have all played their part in creating the amazing scenery that so many people enjoy.

Find out more by visiting www.lochabergeopark.org.uk

Chapter 2

Ancient History and Archaeology

Seann Eachdraidh 's Àrceolas

above:
This dramatic landscape, around the Glen Nevis road end, is rich
with archaeological remains including charcoal burners' platforms

GLEN NEVIS IS rich in history and stories which give a fascinating insight into the lives of the people who lived here. The name 'Nevis' itself has a number of possible origins. One interpretation of the Gaelic place name 'nibheis' or 'nemhais' means 'the venomous one' (and in certain weather conditions Ben Nevis itself may seem exactly that).

It could also come from the Gaelic word 'neb' which means to 'burst or flow' or from an Old Irish word 'neamhaise' meaning 'terrible'. Perhaps all these words have a ring of truth about them and failure to pin down any precise meaning simply adds to the intrigue of this remarkable landscape.

The stories behind the archaeology

Did you know:
Archaeologists working in the glen have to date discovered 43 archaeological sites including settlements, boundary walls or fences, charcoal burners' platforms, tracks and paths.

You don't have to be an historian or archaeologist to learn about the stories hidden in the landscape. Here is a quick and simple guide to some of the best known sites in Glen Nevis, where you can see them and a little bit about their history.

Dun Deardail

This iron-age fort is of national importance and the walk to it begins at Glen Nevis Visitor Centre. Dun Deardail sits on a hill overlooking the glen – the ideal defensive location for a fort – and is thought to have been built in the 7th century BC.

At that time the glen would have looked very different to the view we get today with the surrounding slopes densely covered with trees.

Dun Deardail is a vitrified fort – a name given to stone enclosures where the surrounding walls were fused together by fire. Vitrified forts are particularly interesting because nobody really knows how they were built or how the stone became vitrified.

There have been a number of attempts to try and reproduce vitrification including one in Glen Nevis itself in 2001. The group, led by the Lochaber Hisorical Society, and including a Nevis Ranger and workers from Rio Tinto Alcan, managed to get the temperature up to 1700 degrees celsius, but despite this intense heat the stone still failed to vitrify.

Dun, Dige

Dun Dige is a medieval earthwork near Glen Nevis House. It is believed to have once been the home of the MacSorlie chiefs, a now extinct branch of Clan Cameron.

It was from here, so the story goes, that men from Clan Chattan took their dreadful and bloody revenge on Clan Cameron. The word 'dige' is the Gaelic form of dyke which is either a ditch or wall.

Ach Nan Con burial ground

Easy to spot, this burial ground is a wonderfully scenic place at the foot of the west slope of Ben Nevis and surrounded by old trees.

Close to the burial ground is an old settlement which is thought to date from between 1755 and 1845. The settlement has been almost completely buried by flood debris but you can still see one good house and an excellent corn drying kiln.

The place name, Ach Nan Con, remains a puzzle. It means 'Field of the Dogs'. It might mean that the settlement itself was once used for dog kennels. Quite why the same name was chosen for the burial ground is a mystery.

Blar Bhan Farmstead

You'll find this house and enclosed arable field on the south bank of the River Nevis downstream from the Gorge. This large, well-built though dilapidated square-cornered house, which was built sometime before the 1870s, is easy to reach.

Clach Shomairle – Wishing Stone

The name Clach Shomairle means Stone of Sumerled or Samuel. This massive stone was probably transported by a glacier millions of years ago. Archaeologists call this kind of rock a 'glacial erratic'.

As with so many things in Glen Nevis, this is a stone with a story. According to WT Kilgour's book 'Lochaber in War and Peace' the stone 'was placed in its present position (near the Braveheart Car Park) to commemorate a decisive victory by a chieftain of the Sliochd Shomairle Ruaidh, from whom the Camerons of Glen Nevis derived their patronymic of 'MacSorlie'.'

Another local legend states that at certain points in the year this stone, weighing at least fifty tons, turns three times. Anyone who sees the stone in motion will receive answers to any questions they have.

Somerled's Cave – Uamh Shomairle

This cave is associated with countless tales and legends. It lies just above Blar Bhan Farmstead mentioned above, but if you're planning to explore this cave, you'll need to be careful. The entrance is hard to find and is best approached from above and to the side, it then opens up to a chamber ranging from six to fifteen feet high. At the far end are two passages one of which goes underground.

Somerled's Cave is said to have provided crucial refuge for Glen Nevis Camerons on at least two occasions; once after the massacre of the clan at Dun Dige by the Mackintoshes and again when Glen Nevis House was raided by Cumberland's troops in 1746.

The Camerons are also believed to have fled into the cave while on the run from a raiding expedition.

The cave is also linked by legend to Ossian, a Gaelic bard who was supposed to have lived during the 3rd century.

Upper Steall Settlement

Families lived in this remote part of Glen Nevis until well after the turn of the 1900s. The walk up to Steall needs to be done with care but it is well worth the visit.

Old Steall House itself is a large, stone house with a number of enclosures attached to it which were probably used as sheep handling pens.

The house, now in a very dilapidated condition, but rooved and very likely still inhabited in the 1920s, had three distinct living areas. The gable wall facing east is the best preserved and stands – rather precariously – 2.80m high

There is also a small area of rig and furrow which was a method of farming practised in more mountainous areas of the UK. This technique, which creates a corrugated effect on the land, helped carry away excess water by creating raised areas of cultivation and furrows.

photographs, right
The old cemetery (top) and
Meal Cumhann, Glen Nevis

Charcoal burners' platforms

During the late 18th century timber from a number of places – including Glen Nevis - was bought by the Lorne Furnace Company in Bonawe in Argyll to use in iron smelting.

The charcoal was probably bought 'readymade' after having been manufactured on the many charcoal burners' platforms which exist in Glen Nevis. The best examples lie on the steep slopes on both sides of the River Nevis

between the Lower Falls and the Nevis Gorge.

Archaeologists have, so far, uncovered a total of 48 platforms at this site and it's highly likely there are more waiting to be discovered.

There are some other impressive platforms on the south side of the river, where you can still see the stone revetments which were built to protect the slopes from erosion.

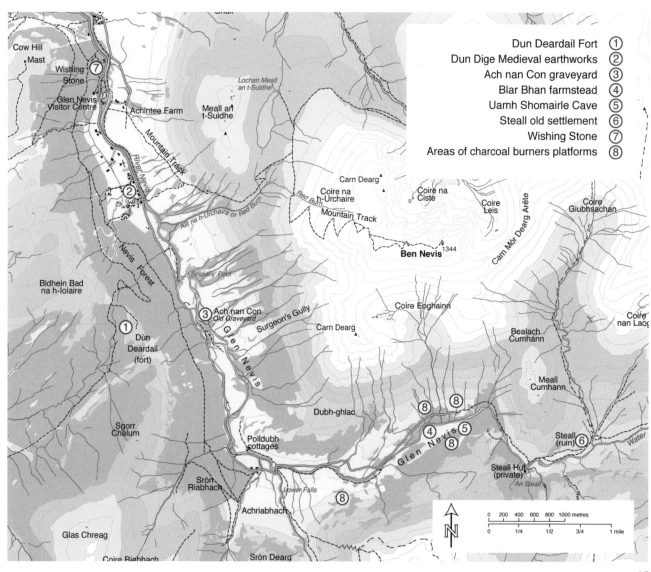

Dun Deardail Fort	①
Dun Dige Medieval earthworks	②
Ach nan Con graveyard	③
Blar Bhan farmstead	④
Uamh Shomairle Cave	⑤
Steall old settlement	⑥
Wishing Stone	⑦
Areas of charcoal burners platforms	⑧

left: The inside of the Ben Nevis Hotel
right: Farmstead, Glen Nevis

Social and clan history

Eachdraidh Cinnidh 's Soisealta

A pioneering people

ON JUNE 2nd 1953 a small group of adults and school children walked through the pouring rain carrying bundles of wood and slowly made their way up the track to the top of Ben Nevis.

Their purpose was to build a bonfire to mark the Coronation of Elizabeth II. The rain – as it often does – kept falling and it was simply too wet to do anything on the summit of the Ben but to turn around and walk back down again.

In many ways this story serves as a kind of symbol of life in the Glen: a life lived on the margins but one which was full and rich (although not necessarily materially). It was a life where, whatever the weather, you kept going.

Glen Nevis has a long, though not necessarily continuous, history of occupation.

The earliest documentary record of the glen that we know of is most probably the 1456 Charter which states that John of Islay, Lord of the Isles, granted the 'lands of Glenyves' to Shomairle, a founder of the MacSorlie clan which was a branch (also known as a 'sept') of Clan Cameron.

There are large swathes of time where history is silent and very little is known of life in the Glen.

But what we do know provides an unforgettable insight into life in one of Scotland's most beautiful glens.

The Ben Nevis Observatory

What better place to really get to grips with the weather than on the top of Britain's highest mountain?

This was the view of a group of amateur meteorologists who in 1883 opened the first and only observatory on the summit of Ben Nevis.

The cost of construction, including all the equipment, was the equivalent of £198,000 in today's money. The path leading up to the top – and the one used today by the majority of visitors starting from the farm in Achintee – cost £12,693.

The Observatory was an extraordinary feat to have achieved. Building work took place in the most extremes of weathers. Materials, when they couldn't be carried by men, were taken up the track by pony and the track itself was built in just four months using local labour.

The Ben Nevis Observatory was manned continuously for 21 years and finally closed in 1904.

You can still see the Observatory's remains to the south of the summit.

Did you know

Two years after the Observatory was built, a small hotel opened on the top of Ben Nevis. It was open for business during the summer months. Lunch was three shillings and bed and breakfast ten shillings. It closed in 1916.

opposite page
top: The Ben Nevis Observatory
below: Rubbish tipping from the old observatory - down Gardyloo Gully

from top:
The curling ponds in Glen Nevis in the 1890s
Original Steall Bridge, at head of Nevis Gorge
Entrance to Glen Nevis at the turn of the 20th century

SUSPENSION BRIDGE,
HEAD OF GLEN NEVIS, FORT WILLIAM

Living in the Glen

Much of what we know of life in Glen Nevis during the last 100 years or so has been gleaned from the memories of people who lived here.

At the far end of Glen Nevis lie the Nevis Gorge and Steall Falls. The last people to live in this remote and beautiful valley would have moved out in the 1930s. A cottage from that time still stands and is used today as a climbing bothy.

With no school or shop, every Monday the children would set out and walk the three-and-a-half miles to Achriabhach for their lessons. They would stay there until Friday and then return home.

Food and other essential provisions would be walked through the gorge. It was a simple, unspoilt life.

During the 1950s most people living in Glen Nevis had their homes around the area of Glen Nevis Farm. It was the obvious place to choose mainly because it was close to the youth hostel, the farm itself and houses and cottages which the Forestry Commission had built for workers and their families.

In this close little community those with land around their homes would keep poultry and grow vegetables. There was also venison from the hill, which families would share out, and even the occasional salmon from the River Nevis.

What they couldn't grow or make themselves using the fresh milk, cream and butter from the farm was brought into the Glen by mobile shops.

Household rubbish was collected once a week by horse and cart and, for a treat, local children would often hitch a ride.

A number of enterprising people opened up small teashops. One of the now deserted cottages at Achriabhach was home to one of these and was run by a local shepherd.

Further down the glen towards Fort William were the Croft Tearooms, situated next to the curling ponds. Not only did it serve up hot meals and ice cream but it also provided the perfect venue for Saturday night dances.

Curling was a hugely popular sport and a great way for people to get together. This was where the Fort William Curling Club met. The club is now 140 years old and continues to meet but no longer uses the ponds in Glen Nevis.

The old curling ponds in Glen Nevis are worth a visit. After turning into the glen, drive for about half a mile and then look for a small parking area on the left hand side. Walk a few metres back to the gate to reach the pond. The Nevis Partnership is leading a project to landscape the area.

Did you know:
Electricity first came to Glen Nevis in 1952

this page:
Top: R. R. Mclan's illustration of a Cameron, 1845.
Bottom: A Victorian depiction of the medieval massacre of the Glen Nevis Camerons - the MacSorlies.

Clan Cameron

Pride, passion, mystery, battles and feuds. You'll find it all in the fascinating life and times of Clan Cameron who, for many years, had an ancestral stronghold in Glen Nevis.

There are numerous stories and legends linked to this famous clan. Here are just two of the better known ones.

The great escape

It was a night nobody would forget. When the chief of the MacSorlie clan – a now extinct branch of Clan Cameron - invited his arch rivals the Clan Chattan to a conference at his home in Glen Nevis the air was thick with tension.

For a start, the Glen Nevis Camerons were uneasy. As their greatest enemies, surely an evening with the Clan Chattan was tantamount to supping with the devil?

MacSorlie intended the conference to be for peace making purposes. And to begin with things went well.

Gathered at the MacSorlie's home on Dun Dige both sides tucked into some traditional Highland hospitality.

But then MacSorlie made a tactical error. As the Chattans prepared to leave MacSorlie called his piper to play them on their way. The piper's choice of tune – the war pibroch of Clan Cameron - was deliberately provocative.

The Clan Chattan members were furious. Determined to make the Camerons pay, the party held a conference of their own at a place which lies just inside the entrance to the holiday park known as Cnocan-na-mi-Chomhairle (The Hill of Evil Counsel).

Shortly after midnight the men of Clan Chattan returned to Dun Dige to reap their bloody revenge. Men, women and children were killed and the stronghold itself set alight.

The only person to escape was a young man called Iain MacDhom'ic Raoil. He fled taking with him a baby boy – the heir of the Glen Nevis Camerons. For the first few weeks he and the child hid in a nearby cave until, still fearing for his safety, he fled further north.

And here he and the boy stayed for many years until it was safe to return home and the boy – now a young man – could take up his rightful place as Chief of the MacSorlies of Glen Nevis.

This incident is thought to have occurred some time after 1386. Feuding between clans happened frequently and the Camerons were no exception.

Clan Cameron after Culloden

Glen Nevis was an important Clan Cameron (or MacSorlies as they were then called) base. Not surprisingly therefore, the glen itself became the focus of opposition of all that the clan stood for.

The Clan Cameron was the biggest supporter of Bonnie Prince Charlie. Under their chief, Donald of Lochiel, they had already attempted a failed siege on Fort William starting on 20th March 1746 and ending on 3 April.

That campaign was planned and run from Glen Nevis House but strong resistance from the English soon had the Cameron men heading back to the hills.

Then just a couple of weeks later came Culloden and its brutal aftermath. Clan Cameron members were labelled as rebels, hunted down in their Glen Nevis stronghold by the Duke of Cumberland and his men and shown no mercy. Glen Nevis House was badly damaged by Hanoverian troops and many Camerons left the glen.

Today, the modern day home of the Camerons of Glen Nevis is the beautiful Glen Nevis House which was rebuilt after 1746.

Camerons still live in Glen Nevis and now run thriving businesses based on tourism and farming.

Chapter 4

Cànan 's Cultar

Language and Culture

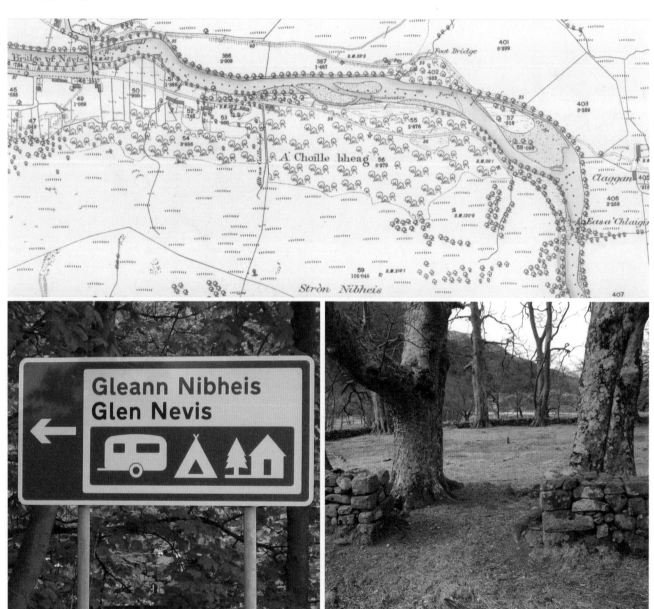

Gaelic – a deep and ancient language

IF YOU WANT to understand how one of Europe's oldest languages found its way into the Highlands of Scotland you need to look west and across the sea to Ireland.

Exactly how long Gaelic has been spoken in Scotland is hard to pin down, but what is known is that it arrived on Scottish shores with settlers from County Antrim in Ireland looking to expand the Irish sea kingdom of Dalriada.

The first stopping off point for these Irish migrants was 6th century Argyll. But they had not arrived in an empty or undefended country.

Parts of Scotland at that time were inhabited by the Picts, a mysterious, fighting people whose strongholds tended to be in the north and east of Scotland.

Nevertheless, slowly but surely as the kingdom of Dalriada began to expand further into Scotland - or Alba as the Irish called it – so too did the Gaelic language.

By the 9th century the rule and reign of the Picts was declining and the new Kingdom of Alba was being promoted, with Gaelic as the language of the king and court.

The language and its culture continued to prosper. During the 12th, 13th and 14th centuries, great Gaelic families such as Clann Dòmhnaill began to make their mark, ruling as Lords of the Isles for more than 200 years.

A move to the margins

But the journey of this language across Scotland began to falter and soon it encountered a series of challenges which would, eventually, erode much of its position and influence.

The kings of Scotland might have boasted of their Gaelic lineage, but in reality they barely gave a thought to its future.

As different religious structures were introduced and new trade routes opened up, the people making these changes were lowland Scots who spoke Inglis.

This was, to all intents and purposes, an English dialect. Gaelic would have been utterly incomprehensible to Inglis speakers. These changes were a heavy blow to Gaelic so that by the 14th and 15th centuries it was Inglis, not Gaelic, which had muscled its way through to become the official language of the law.

The battle of Culloden in 1746 and its terrible, repressive aftermath drove Gaelic even further to the margins. The traditional clan system went into decline as did its culture and language.

Because Glen Nevis was strongly Jacobite, people living here would have felt the full force of the wave of violence and terror which swept through the Highlands as government troops pursued their relentless campaign to wipe out Jacobite supporters.

The final decades of the 19th century brought a further blow and it came from the direction of education.

There had been some early experiments in Gaelic-medium education, but with the introduction of the Education Act of 1872 English was made the sole medium of teaching.

As elsewhere in the Highlands, children in Glen Nevis brought up with Gaelic as their first language, suddenly found themselves being punished at school for uttering a single word in their mother tongue.

By now Gaelic was largely confined to the family and the church. In Glen Nevis, it was still being spoken widely in the 1940s and even in the 1960s there were still Gaelic speakers living in the glen – mainly the older forestry workers.

Today there is only one known gaelic speaker living in the glen. Gaelic, once the main language in Glen Nevis, has become a language on the edge.

above
A fresh wave of Gaelic music and song is helping pull the Gaelic language back from the edge.

opposite page
top: By the 1870s the language of the cartographer was English, although as this 1876 Ordnance Survey map demonstrates, place names continued to be in Gaelic and still are to this day
bottom left: modern bi-lingual road sign
bottom right: entrance to the old graveyard at Ach nan Con

Back from the brink?

It's strange how some of the most fragile things can also be the most resilient.

Recent years have seen a determined push to ensure the Gaelic language does not vanish. Gaelic was given new status as an official language in Scotland, commanding equal respect with English, with the introduction of the Gaelic Language Bill in April 2005.

The bill also established Bòrd na Gàidhlig which today has a key role to promote Gaelic in Scotland, advising Scottish Ministers on Gaelic issues, driving forward Gaelic planning and preparing guidance on Gaelic education.

Gaelic in schools is beginning to flourish – around 3,600 young people study Gaelic as a subject in secondary schools and there are nearly 2000 children who attend Gaelic-medium pre-schools.

above right
The annual Fèis Lochabair msic festival is helping secure the future of Gaelic culture.

Gaelic culture, music and song

There is something mysterious and magical about Gaelic. When spoken the words have an elemental quality – you can almost hear wind, waves and water.

Not surprisingly perhaps, Gaelic has a vibrant story-telling tradition; stories which would capture the ordinary lives of people going about their every day tasks – weaving, rowing, milking the cow - and be passed down from generation to generation.

These stories would find their way into songs, music and poetry that would capture the full range of human experience, from birth to death.

Today, there is a fresh wave of Gaelic music and song which is helping to pull this language back from the margins and keeping it alive.

The Blas Festival ('blas' is Gaelic for 'taste') has become an annual music event showcasing some of the best of traditional music and Gaelic in the Highlands.

The Lochaber area has a rich vein of musical talent with fiddlers such as Aonghas Grant, Allan Henderson and Iain MacFarlane making it onto the world stage.

The future of musical talent in the region is also being encouraged with the help of Fèis Lochabair, which holds year round musical activities and events for children.

Some things you might not know about Gaelic

Gaelic is part of the Goidelic (Q) Celtic languages along with Irish and Manx. Speakers of any of these languages can, in part at least, understand each other.

At one time Gaelic was the main language in Scotland. It was spoken from Caithness in the north down to Galloway in the south and from Fraserburgh in the East to St. Kilda in the west.

In the 2001 Census there was 58,652 Gaelic Speakers in Scotland.

Forced migration meant hundreds of people left their homes in the Highlands. Many ended up in Canada and, at the time of the Canadian Confederation in 1867, Gaelic was the country's third most spoken language. As many as one hundred thousand Nova Scotians spoke Gaelic as their mother tongue in 1900.

Today there are thought to be between 1000 and 2000 Gaelic speakers in Nova Scotia.

A number of communities in Quebec were settled by Gaelic-speaking emigrants from Lochaber.

Gaelic speakers and learners can be found all over the world including Patagonia, Brazil, Australia, New Zealand, Europe and Russia. And in the days of the British Empire many native Gaelic speakers were born in places such as India.

Gaelic place names in Glen Nevis and how you say them

Dun Deardail (Doon Jee-ar-dull)
Deidre's Fort. Named after Deirdre from celtic mythology who, legend says, caused the death of the three heroes of Ulster.

Dun Dige (Doon Jee-guh)
Ditch/Dyke Fort. This is the site of the original home of the MacSorlies. It would have been a wooden structure surrounded by a moat or ditch.

Uamh Shomhairle (Oo-av Hoh-orl-yuh)
Samuel's Cave. This cave has been used as a place of refuge in the past by the Camerons on at least two occasions.

Carn Dearg (Carn Jarag)
Red Rocky Mountain

Sgorr an Iubhair (Skorr un Ewe-ur)
Mountain of the Yew

Am Bodach (Am Bot-uch)
The Old Man

Poll Dubh (Pow-ul Doo)
Black Pool

Coire an Lochain (Corr-uh un Loch-un)
Coire of the Little Loch

Stob Bàn (Stop Bah-un)
Fair or White Hill

An Steall (Un Shhh-chee-al)
The Spout (waterfall)

Meall an t-suidhe (Mee-yal un Too-yuh)
Hill of the Seat. Perhaps confusingly, the area under the hill is known as Dail an t-sithidh (Field of the Stormy Blast) leading some people to speculate that the original name for the hill is Meall an t-sìthidh (Mee-yal un Chee).

Chapter 5

Industry and farming in the Glen

Gnìomhachas 's Tuathanachas

below Aerial view of Rio Tinto Alcan's Lochaber Smelter with Meall an t-Suidhe in the background.
opposite Lochaber smelter powerhouse, prior to recent renovation

The land in Glen Nevis serves a multitude of purposes. That may seem a rather odd statement when, on the surface, it might appear that this region of mountains, peaks, rivers and steep valley walls could offer very little in the way of industry.

But the glen has a subterranean industrial heart which has been steadily beating away for more than 90 years.

Aluminium – power from the hills

RAIN. THERE'S PLENTY of it in the Highlands. But if it hadn't been for the guaranteed abundance of this renewable resource the aluminium industry – which plays a vital role in the region's economy – would probably never have happened.

It was in the 1890s that generating electricity using water power really started to take off. The Highlands of Scotland was the perfect place for this new industry to be born. It had lots of rain and plenty of big mountains.

At the same time, another fledgling industry was finding its feet – aluminium smelting. The one thing which aluminium production needs is large amounts of cheaply produced electricity, which is exactly what it found in hydro electric power, and, in the Highlands, the water needed to produce this electricity is an infinite resource. It was the abundance of water in the Ben Nevis area which made it such an ideal location for aluminium production.

The Lochaber smelter itself, where the aluminium is still manufactured today, was built in Fort William in 1929. It was the third smelter that the British Aluminium Company had built in the area. The first was in Foyers in 1896 followed by Kinlochleven in 1909.

There was widespread support for the Lochaber smelter. It provided a crucial boost to an area which had been in decline, having already lost 17 per cent of its population to immigration.

But before the Lochaber smelter opened, there was vital work to be done to ensure a constant supply of water. Getting the water required a 15 mile long, 4.6 metre diameter tunnel to be built beneath the mountains and right through the northern flank of the Ben Nevis range. It took 2,000 men three years to complete. It was highly dangerous work too. Fatal and non-fatal accidents happened on an almost daily basis.

But the result was extraordinary. Even by today's standards this tunnel was a massive feat of engineering. When the Lochaber smelter was modernised in the 1980s there was a chance to inspect the tunnel for the first time in 29 years. It was found to be in remarkably good condition and needed just a few, minor repairs, a testament to the skills of the men who built it

The tunnel begins by taking water from remote Loch Treig, which lies to the east of Glen Nevis, and ends at the smelter in Fort William. Here you can clearly see the vast pipelines, which run 600 feet down the hillside to the hydro station.

The opening of the Lochaber smelter came just in time for the Second World War, which highlighted the importance of aluminium for military and civil uses.

Aluminium remains integral to life in Glen Nevis. Rio Tinto Alcan is a major land owner in the area and, if it were possible to find the perfect industry for such a wild place, aluminium has to be it. Not only does it harness resources which already exist but, because of the underground tunnel, much of it remains hidden from view.

Did you know
The Rio Tinto Alcan smelter in Fort William produces 43,000 tonnes of aluminium each year and contributes £8m to the local economy. It employs 173 people directly but at least twice that number locally who provide support and services.

Its power house once had the largest net output of any hydro electric installation in the UK.

The aluminium made at Fort William is transported to Rio Tinto Alcan rolling mills elsewhere in the UK and Europe.

below The start of the tunnel, first built in the 1920s, which took water from Loch Treig to the smelter at Fort William.

Forestry – a changing industry

The community in Glen Nevis grew up around one main industry – forestry. Like many things, forestry has had to adapt and change over the years but as recently as 30 years ago the glen was considered a forest district in its own right.

It was a tight-knit community, with its own Head Forester, a small office and it provided much needed jobs for local people.

The Forestry Commission was set up between the first and second world wars to address the serious shortfall in home grown timber.

This raised the very real question of exactly where this much-needed timber resource was to come from. The answer was to buy areas of land so that new forests could be established. Glen Nevis, together with other areas across the whole of Scotland, was chosen as just such a place.

With its steep slopes and rocky ground, Glen Nevis presented quite a challenge to those early foresters and planting and fencing would have been very labour intensive.

In the 1960s and '70s the forestry industry had to change again. With the demand for home grown timber dropping, the Forestry Commission had to think more creatively about its role. What other uses might forests have for people?

This important question opened up a new role for the Forestry Commission. New work was begun to improve the actual appearance of forests in the glen; paths and tracks were developed for visitors and important work was started – and which continues - looking at ways to protect native woodland habitants.

Today, the Forestry Commission's key role is managing the Glen Nevis forest to support local timber processing. However, this work is set against a complex background where the demands on the forest have changed significantly.

With tens of thousands of visitors coming to the glen every year, forestry workers have to rise to the challenge of getting timber to the roadside safely.

With so many pairs of feet walking through the glen, there is also a need to ensure the network of paths and car parks are kept in good condition.

There is also vital work going on in the area of conservation. An ancient woodland site in the upper reaches of the forest is being restored and key wildlife species including the red squirrel and the chequered skipper butterfly are being safeguarded.

Did you know
Forestry Commission Scotland (FCS) owns 2,357 acres (954 ha) in Glen Nevis

Farming in Glen Nevis

Before the days of forestry and aluminium, it was farming which was once central to life in Glen Nevis.

The nature of the landscape meant the glen was used almost exclusively for grazing cattle and sheep. Arable crops on any large scale would never have survived here although the outlines of old 'lazy beds' – which you can see on the east side of the River Nevis just upstream from the Youth Hostel – are evidence that some small areas of land would have been cultivated.

'Lazy beds' was a way of growing crops that was widely used in Scotland until the 19th century. It involved digging rows of ridges and furrows and gave the land a distinctive ribbed or corrugated appearance.

Farming was not an industry for the faint hearted. Shepherds would walk miles and in all weathers to gather their black faced sheep, a breed chosen for its ability to survive in an unforgiving climate.

Half a century ago there would have been around 1400 sheep in the glen. While these numbers have fallen sharply in recent years sheep are still bred and they remain an important part of life in this unique area for one important reason – grazing.

Without sheep, the land would not be grazed and scrub would quickly start to invade the glen making it very difficult for walkers and other visitors to have the easy access they do today.

Cattle are still bred in the glen and there is real pride in the pedigree herd of Highland cattle, which includes the 'old type' black breed. Stalking and fishing take place on a relatively small scale on Ben Nevis, and in Glen Nevis.

Like forestry, farming has also had to adapt to a world that is changing. Farmers in the glen have successfully diversified into other areas, mainly tourism and conservation, where they play a key role in helping preserve and protect this special landscape - a commitment born out in a recent joint project with the Glen Nevis Estate, Forestry Commission and Rio Tinto Alcan planting native species of woodland at Achriabhach.

Did you know

Built in 1827 the Ben Nevis Distillery in Fort William is one of the oldest licensed distilleries in Scotland. Its founder, John MacDonald, used water from two small lochans on Ben Nevis in his whisky making.

Top:
Glen Nevis still supports a herd of pedigree Highland cattle.
Bottom:
Black faced sheep

Chapter 6

One big, natural playground

Cur-seachadan

PEAKS, SLOPES, WATER, tracks and trails – they're all here in Glen Nevis making it one of the most exciting natural playgrounds to be found anywhere in the British Isles.

This is a place of extremes, from the dizzying rush of fast-flowing torrents when the River Nevis is in spate to the ice-covered cliffs of Ben Nevis in winter, when it is sought out by climbers from all over the world.

But if speed and height have just a bit too much adrenalin for comfort, there are also some spectacularly beautiful river and forest walks on the lower levels offering easy walking and dramatic scenery.

Whatever your pace, there are many ways to walk, climb, cycle or kayak in Glen Nevis.

Mountaineering & Climbing:

What is it that gets grown men and women out of their beds at unearthly hours, often in sub-zero temperatures, to tackle some of the most difficult routes up Britain's highest mountain?

Ben Nevis remains at the forefront of world mountaineering. There are plenty of higher, more remote peaks in other parts of this planet, but what draws climbers back to the Ben time and time again is the range of climbs it offers – particularly the 700 metre high cliffs on its famous North Face which make it one of the leading places in the UK for ice climbing – and some of the most ferocious and unpredictable weather conditions anywhere in Europe.

On its summit there can be complete white-outs even in June and during the winter months it's not unknown to have to queue to get up some of its crags and gullies.

Climbers will tell you that this is a mountain that gets under your skin. There's just something about its huge hulk and craggy rock faces that gives the mountain a character all of its own.

Mountaineering has changed significantly since James Robertson, an Edinburgh botanist, made the first recorded ascent of Ben Nevis on 17 August 1771.

Climbing in those days was vastly different from today. Dressed in hobnail boots, tweeds – even a collar and tie - and carrying axes and hemp ropes, these early climbers had very little protection and none of the specialist technical clothing mountaineers in the 21st century enjoy.

What drove them on then, as it does climbers today, was an almost overwhelming obsession with this giant of mountains.

The building of the pony track in 1883 for the Ben Nevis summit observatory opened up the first direct route to the top.

It is this same route which today, more than 150,000 people climb to reach the summit of Ben

Nevis. For many, it's the only mountain they may ever climb – a personal Everest.

Then there's that elite group of experienced climbers for whom the main draw are the technically challenging ascents of the Ben's pinnacles, buttresses, ridges and towers and where even today new routes are still being found.

But whatever and however you climb, Ben Nevis commands respect. This is a mountain whose mood can change in an instant with the weather whipping up to a storm when only moments ago the sun had been shining.

For all its popularity, this is a mountain where you need to take care and be prepared.

One of the most popular rock outcrops for climbing in Glen Nevis is Polldubh. Its crags are popular with climbers from all over the UK.

The man to make the first climb at Polldubh more than 60 years ago was Jimmy Ness who lives in Fort William. A pioneer of climbing, Jimmy brought the crags to the attention of other climbers and there are now hundreds of routes there. The Nevis Partnership is working with the local climbing club to help keep this important climbing venue clear of trees and scrub.

Walking up The Ben

The main route up Ben Nevis begins at Achintee, about four miles from the centre of Fort William. Park at the Glen Nevis Visitor Centre and cross the bridge to reach the beginning of the path.

If you're a novice walker please use the main tourist path. You must be reasonably fit, but by walking at a steady pace it should take you between seven to nine hours to reach the summit and back.

You will need to be well equipped. The weather can suddenly change and even in the height of summer the temperature on the top can be below zero. Always take:

- A map and compass
- Wear good walking boots
- Warm clothing and a waterproof jacket and trousers
- Hat and gloves
- Water and something to eat

It's amazing what people throw away – drink bottles, barbecues, tin cans, champagne corks, banana skins (which biodegrade extremely slowly because it's so cold). We've found all that and more on the summit of the Ben. This is a fragile and special environment which needs protection. Every year, volunteers stage an assault on all the rubbish that people throw away, so please, please take yours with you when you leave.

The path climbs steeply to the saddle by Lochan Meall as t-Suidhe before the final ascent on zigzag path up the stony west flank of Ben Nevis.

An alternative route up, and one recommended only for experienced walkers, is via the Carn Mor Deag Arête. This starts at Torlundy at the car park for the North Face of the mountain which is a little further up the A82 out of Fort William.

The summit of Ben Nevis is a massive stony plateau measuring about 90 acres. A large cairn, which sits on top of an Ordnance Survey trig point, marks the highest point.

This is the place for all kinds of weather. But on a good day with clear skies and great visibility the views are out of this world.

Workers for the John Muir Trust, which owns much of the mountain, had a surprise in May 2006, when they uncovered a piano which had been buried under one of the cairns on the peak. It's believed to have been carried up as part of charity event by a team of removals men from Dundee some 20 years earlier.

Running

Not everyone climbs or walks up Ben Nevis. Each year men and women from all parts of the UK and beyond gather at Claggan Park football ground on the outskirts of Fort William to take part in the gruelling Ben Nevis Race – a 14km run with a 1,340 metre ascent to the top of Ben Nevis and back again.

They're following in the footsteps of a man called William Swan, a barber from Fort William, and the first person to make the first recorded hill run of this massive mountain. He did it in 2 hours 41 minutes.

The present day record, from Claggan Park, is almost half Swan's time. This run is not for the fainthearted. Entry is restricted to people who have already completed three hill races and, even then, numbers are kept to a maximum of 500 people due to the fragile and demanding nature of the mountain environment.

Anyone who doesn't make it to the peak in two hours is turned back.

Wild Water

Rain. There can be plenty of it here on the West Coast. But if you love water sports – especially kayaking or canoeing – rain, and the more the better, provides some of the best conditions.

The River Nevis has become a huge attraction for white water sport enthusiasts. But what is it that makes this particular river so special?

Quite simply, it's the abundance of rapids, gorges and tight, twisting channels which makes the Nevis both exciting and unpredictable. ·

The upper section of the river is where the most challenging waters are to be found. With names such as Boulder Blast, the Mad Mile, Leg Breaker and Roaring Mill, these are waters for really experienced canoeists.

Kayakers grade white water on a scale of 1 to 6. Grade 1 rapids are easy while grade 6 enters the realm of the impossible.

The River Nevis almost has it all. There are plenty of grade 4 rapids and some really tough grade 5 runs. In a kayaker's world, this is almost paradise. ·

Ask any white water rider and they'll tell you that one of the most exciting sections starts at the foot of the Nevis gorge and runs down to the Polldubh Falls.

Water like this is for those who really know what they're doing. You can find a gentler ride in the lower sections of the Nevis. Here the waters are less turbulent and the view just as amazing – just watch out for the one major rapid near the end and, if you think it's too much, head for the bank.

If you fancy a dip into icy water on nothing more than an inflatable lilo then the Glen Nevis River Race could be right up your street. The event takes place every summer in the glen and raises thousands of pounds for Lochaber Mountain Rescue Team

Walking & Cycling

You don't have to head for Britain's highest mountain peak to enjoy what Glen Nevis has to offer.

On the lower slopes and along the valley itself are some truly beautiful low levels walks, ideal if you want a gentler, slower route.

There are walks that will take you along the River Nevis, through Glen Nevis Forest with its dense canopy of spruce or tracks and paths that will take you to the ancient iron-age fort of Dun Deardail.

And remember, whatever the weather, it can change very quickly here. However undemanding your walk, we recommend you go prepared with waterproofs, walking boots, food and drinks, sun cream, hat and gloves.

The West Highland Way – Scotland's first official long distance route - links Milngavie on the northern outskirts of Glasgow to Fort William, a distance of 154 km (96 miles). The walk finishes passes the foot of Ben Nevis. Up to 80,000 people walk the West Highland Way every year with around 30,000 completing the route from start to finish.

The road through Glen Nevis is ideal for cycling. From the entrance to the glen the road winds along for about 12 miles. It rises gently and should take you about half a day. The road becomes single track towards the end of the glen and although there are plenty of passing places, things can get a bit busy in the summer months so do take care.

Chapter 7

Natural history in the glen

Nàdair sa Ghleann

BEN NEVIS AND the Glen are widely regarded as one of the best places in Britain for its diversity of wildlife, natural native woodland and unique geology.

It's a landscape of contrasts and extremes from woodlands on the lower levels of the glen to the vast mountainous areas that dominate the skyline.

It is an area that is both rich and fragile in its biodiversity and, consequently, calls for careful, sensitive protection and conservation.

Wet heath and woodlands

High rainfall, altitude, and the ground conditions which are so specific to this area (predominantly acidic soils, limestone in places) all play key roles in making this region so rich in its biodiversity.

On the lower flanks of Ben Nevis and down into the Glen Nevis basin is a moorland landscape known as wet heath. You'll find a lot of this in the West Highlands and it is important for nature conservation as there is so little anywhere else in the world.

Further up Glen Nevis you'll soon see how the abundance of woodland starts to become apparent.

The steep, craggy banks of Nevis Gorge support the most significant area of woodland in the glen which includes birch, rowan, willow with hazel, alder and ash as well as other native species nearer the river bank.

On the south-facing slopes above the Water of Nevis in the upper reaches of Glen Nevis, there is little tree cover but what you will encounter further up the Glen is the native Scots pine, a tree that once grew extensively throughout the ancient and long gone Caledonian Pine Forest.

Today just 1% of the estimated 1,500,000 hectare original forest area remains.

The Scots pine is a hugely important tree and widely regarded as a keystone species in the ecosystem as it forms the 'backbone' on which many other species depend.

The soil in Glen Nevis rarely dries out thanks to the vast number of streams and high rainfall. Combine all this water with the cool oceanic climate and you have the perfect growing conditions for the large number of mosses and liverworts which carpet the forest floor on the sides of Steall Gorge and which are usually visible all year round.

Look out for the many species of 'sphagnum' moss - an incredibly useful plant. Moss has an unusual structure due to its ability to hold water and air inside its cells which it then releases.

All this water makes the moss spongy, keeps it wetter for longer and helps it grow. The water is only released slowly and this makes sphagnum bogs very important for reducing flooding because they absorb heavy rainfall but only release it gradually.

As these wooded areas open up onto moorland

Did you know:
Much of Ben Nevis and Glen Nevis have one or more official conservation designations, of both national (Site of Special Scientific Interest, National Scenic Area) and European importance (Special Area of Conservation).

left
Scots Pine in upper Glen Nevis

The Scots Pine is a hugely important tree and widely regarded as a keystone species in the ecosystem as it forms the 'backbone' on which many other species depend

Did you know:

The River Nevis is a good river to spot the Atlantic Salmon. The best place to see leaping salmon as they travel up river is at Roaring Mill (the little falls just downstream from the Nevis visitor Centre) usually in September.

They spawn here from mid to late October or perhaps into November in the gravels just under the bridge outside the visitor centre.The Lower Falls ensure the salmon do not journey any further up the Glen. Brown trout, sea trout and, if you look very closely, eels can also be found on this stretch of the river.

this then becomes ideal habitat for heathers. There are three main types of heather that grow here - bell heather, cross-leaved heath and ling – and all of them are an important food source for many birds in early spring.

Wild flowers grow in abundance in the glen during the spring and summer. Look out for:

■ Primroses which you'll find scattered around the Glen in early spring

■ Butterworts and Sundews. These trap midges, amongst other insects, and are found throughout the summer in acidic boggy and wet areas.

■ Devils-bit Scabious with its unique late summer Caledonian purple and blue flower. This grows in the glen until the end of the summer season.

■ the bright yellow four-petalled flower of Tormentil. Its nectar attracts the adult Scotch Argus butterfly.

All creatures great and small

The largest animal you're likely to encounter in Glen Nevis is the red deer generally found in the upper part of the Glen in Coire Giubhsachan, around Meall Cumhann and in Coire nan Each to the west.

You might also catch sight of it over most of the southern slopes of Ben Nevis. Management of the deer population is crucially important in helping maintain optimum levels of grazing for areas of native woodland regeneration.

Feeding signs of red squirrel have been spotted in the Steall woodlands on the bank of the River Nevis and in the woodland around Polldubh.

Pine marten are present lower down in Glen Nevis and there is evidence they may also be on the southern slopes of Aonach Beag up beyond the Steall ruins.

Badgers, foxes and mink are also resident in Glen Nevis. And if you keep your eyes peeled along the lower stretches of the River Nevis you might even be lucky enough to catch sight of one of the most elusive of British mammals – the otter.

Of the smaller mammals, there is evidence of field voles and sightings of pygmy shrew up in the banks of Steall Gorge, and water voles have been recorded in the upper part of Glen Nevis.

There are bats too (the common pipistrelle and Daubenton's) which, around dusk, feed on insects over the summer time around the Nevis Water at the visitor centre. Pipistrelles have also been seen at Steall.

There are a large number of different species of moth which you can see both day and night in the glen. These include the nationally scarce Exile/Northern Arches moth.

The Glen is also a favourite haunt for dragonflies. These amazingly agile insects can often be seen chasing after food over patches of still water.

Look out for the Common Hawker and Golden-Ringed Dragonflies during July through to August.

There are butterflies too, such as the Mountain Ringlet, a rare mountain butterfly, which makes its home higher up on the slopes of Coire nan Laogh. The best time to look out for these is from July to mid October.

Key Bird Facts

The Golden Eagle may be sighted, particularly in the spring, between Steall bridge and Steall ruins and on the slopes heading up North from the ruins.

Dippers, Common Sandpipers and Goosanders are found on Nevis water courses.

Ring Ouzels, Meadow Pipits, and Stonechats occupy open ground and moorland, and higher still Snow Bunting and Ptarmigan can be found.

Top line, left to right
Eggar Moth caterpillar; Rowan tree at Steall Falls; Golden-ringed Dragonfly

Middle line, left to right
Long-leaved Sundew; Scots Pine young sapling; Red Deer calf

Botton line, left to right
Gorse flowering; Bell Heather in flower; Otter

Chapter 8

Natural history
on the Ben

Nàdar air a' Bheinn

BEN NEVIS AND the peaks surrounding Glen Nevis support an outstanding wealth of wildlife, quite distinct from that in the glen and superbly adapted to the very different conditions which occur there.

As you climb out of the glen, the vegetation changes. You'll find heather as an almost constant companion but many plants, such as bracken, disappear and new ones take over as you approach the high tops. In fact, with a bit of practice, you can judge your altitude surprisingly well by these changes.

Trees struggle to grow above about 500 m though rowan is perhaps the hardiest species –solitary trees can be spotted on crags well above this altitude. Look too for juniper – in high rocky places a special form called prostrate juniper hugs the ground to avoid the wind.

Bushes of the rare downy willow are a special feature of the Ben on high crags whilst the smallest of all the willows, least willow, which is just a few centimetres high, creeps across windswept ridges and summits.

Heather and its relatives, aptly known as dwarf-shrubs, come into their own on the high hills. Like heather, blaeberry or bilberry, as it is also called, flourishes right up the slopes, but is joined higher up by five other berry-bearing shrubs. Crowberry has shiny black berries and is one of the toughest species growing on summit plateaus.

Alpine bearberry is the rarest of these but is readily spotted late in the year when it turns a spectacular fiery red before shedding its leaves. All these berries provide a feast for birds and animals in the autumn.

Life in extremes

The climate changes dramatically with increasing height above sea level, and it doesn't get any higher in Britain than the top of Ben Nevis. Here extreme temperatures, frequent mists and fierce winds combine with rocky terrain and shallow soils to make conditions inhospitable to most plants - yet there is life up here!

Perhaps the most noticeable plant on the top of the Ben and nearby summits is woolly fringe-moss, which forms a soft broken carpet over these rock-strewn plateaus.

Each leaf of this olive-green moss ends in a long white hair. These are thought to help prevent it from drying out and being scorched, two of the main challenges in this hostile, tundra-like environment. Remarkably, mosses such as this can dry out for long periods, and then quickly recover when it rains to continue growing.

These rocky mountains are also home to a wealth of lichens. Lichens are specialised types of fungi that have microscopic plants (algae) embedded within them. In the glen, the trees are typically draped with 'frilly' lichens, but on high ground other types form colourful crusts that cover rock surfaces.

Ben Nevis and the surrounding peaks, including Aonach Beag, the Grey Corries and the Mamores, are renowned for their mountain flowers. These 'arctic-alpines' are brilliantly adapted to live in the harsh conditions of mountain ridges, crags and slopes.

Plants to look out for

Alpine Lady's Mantle: One of the commonest mountain plants which grows beside most of the hill paths. It has yellowish flowers in tiny clusters, but is best recognised by its leaves which are each divided into five or more 'fingers'.

Moss Campion: Less common with numerous pink flowers appearing around June. Like several other arctic-alpines it grows as a wind-resistant domed cushion densely packed with flowers to attract pollinating insects.

Saxifrages: These appear in abundance and up to eight different species are recorded as growing in these mountains. The name saxifrage means 'rock breaker', referring to the fact that some species grow in narrow cracks in rocks.

The most common species is the Starry saxifrage with its pretty white flowers. It grows in mossy mountain springs and on wet rocks – you can see it beside the main path up the Ben. Yellow mountain saxifrage is also common in wet stony places, and has bright yellow flowers, often with red dots.

The most striking species is purple saxifrage. The bell-like, deep pink or purplish flowers appear in March and April, long before most other mountain plants. It grows especially on wet rocks which are rich in lime, such as on Meall Cumhann and Aonach Beag.

Arctic Mouse-ear and Alpine Forget-me-not: These are some of the rarest plants and grow on cliff ledges in inaccessible places such as the east face of the Ben and on Aonach Beag.

Globe flower and Wood Crane's-bill: Wider ledges support colourful, lush growths of these two plants.

Parsley Fern: Banks of mobile scree occur widely on the Ben and might seem an unlikely place for plant life, but even here the parsley fern and other ferns flourish, along with lichens and mosses.

An important habitat on Ben Nevis is the late snowbeds, where snow remains well into the summer. In these areas specific sedges, mosses and tiny liverworts grow, including many rare species. There is concern that climate change may pose a threat to this habitat and monitoring is being carried out.

Top line left to right
Parsley Fern; Purple Saxifrage; Roseroot in flower

Middle line left to right
Snow Bunting; Palmate Newt; Ptarmigan

Bottom line left to right
Crowberry with fruits; Crutose lichens; Woolly Fringe Moss

Fauna

Despite the often high winds, many insects and spiders frequent the high ground on the Ben. Crane-flies can be abundant and are an important food for birds. The mountain ringlet, one of Britain's rarer butterflies, breeds in high corries above Glen Nevis. The emperor moth and the northern eggar can also be seen flying over the hillsides – look for their distinctive caterpillars feeding on heather.

On blaeberry and heather flowers you might also see the uncommon blaeberry bumblebee with its rich orange tail.

Common frogs are plentiful on the Ben, feeding on invertebrates and laying spawn during March wherever there are shallow pools, even at very high altitude.

Another amphibian breeding in these high places is the palmate newt. The male has a distinctive filament at the end of its tail.

The mountain tops and slopes, cliffs and corries are also home to a number of hardy bird species.

The meadow pipit is probably the commonest bird on high ground in summer. Listen for the male's evocative song during its display. The singing bird rises up in the air with a fluttering flight then glides slowly down with wings held out and tail spread.

The snow bunting is one of Scotland's rarest breeding birds, but there is a good chance of seeing one on Ben Nevis. They are surprisingly tame and it is possible to approach them quite closely. The male is unmistakeable at breeding time with pied plumage - predominantly white, and black wing tips, back and tail.

Ring ouzels visit the high corries in summer to breed. This bird is closely related to the blackbird – in fact it is sometimes known as the 'mountain blackbird' (ouzel is the old English name for the blackbird). Like its cousin, the male ring ouzel is black with a yellow beak but can be instantly recognised by a large white crescent across its breast – the 'ring' of its name. In late summer our ring ouzels head south to spend the winter eating juniper berries in the Saharan Atlas mountains.

The ptarmigan is probably one of the toughest birds in Britain. Not only does it breed on the high slopes and summits of our mountains but, unlike most other birds which do so, it chooses to remain there through the winter.

Only heavy snow seems to drive ptarmigan onto to slightly lower slopes. It is a master of disguise, as the only British bird to turn white in winter. The wings remain white all year and the tail black, but the remaining plumage changes from mottled grey-brown in summer, matching its stony habitat, to white in winter, blending with the snowy, frosted landscape.

Ravens are often seen on the high tops. The raven has completely black plumage and black legs. In flight the tips of the wings are splayed out like a buzzard, which is of similar size. The principle call of the raven is a deep, distinctive 'cronk cronk'.

The largest resident bird of prey is the magnificent golden eagle which glides effortlessly overhead looking for food. Others you might see include the tiny merlin and the fastest of all, the peregrine.

Despite the harsh conditions several species of mammals also frequent the high slopes. Red deer are the most conspicuous, moving to high ground in summer to avoid the flies.

Less obvious is the mountain hare, well known for changing its colour during the year. In summer the fur is brown, but with black-tipped ears and a white tail. As the summer progresses it moults to a grey-brown coat; a blue grey under-fur shows through in places, giving its alternative name of blue hare. With the approach of winter the brown fur is quickly moulted leaving a dense, white, winter coat.

You need sharp eyes to spot one, but in winter look for its distinctive Y-shaped tracks in the snow. Its predators include golden eagles and foxes, which commonly travel to high levels for food. Foxes and birds of prey also take short-tailed or field voles which occur frequently on grassy slopes.

Red Deer Stag

Chapter 9

The Ben and Glen Today

A' Bheinn 's An Gleann an-diugh

Nothing ever really stands still – although we may often find ourselves wishing that it might.

One of the key issues those who work or live in Glen Nevis now face is how to strike that crucial balance of promoting one of the most important wild places in the British Isles while, at the same time, protecting it for generations to come.

Perhaps the biggest change to have taken place over the past 50 years or so is the huge growth in tourism.

People come in their thousands and from all over the world to visit this area. Not surprisingly, tourism plays an important role in the local economy.

But what it also brings is added pressure on an already fragile ecological landscape.

150,000 people walk up Ben Nevis each year. And while not everyone will make it to the top that's still an awful lot of feet going up and down this majestic mountain.

This means wear and tear on the paths and there is an ongoing programme to improve the main track to the top, and keep it in good repair.

But the unpredictable weather and the mountain terrain means this is a difficult place to use machinery so most of the Ben Nevis path is built by hand. Hand building also means the path can be built in a style in keeping with the

People come in their thousands and from all over the world to visit this area. Not surprisingly, tourism plays an important role in the local economy.

mountain environment.

This is a tough job involving hard, physical labour. Local stone and gravel is used so that the fragile nature of the ecology is preserved. For path building higher up, the workers live at the Half Way Lochan in cabins which are airlifted in.

Help us protect this special environment

There is also an ongoing battle with rubbish, particularly on the summit of Ben Nevis, which is owned by the John Muir Trust. Several times a year a group of volunteers head to the top to collect the waste that visitors leave behind.

Worse, there is human waste too. A quick toilet break on the plateau of Ben Nevis may be just what's needed after the long haul up but human waste has a hugely detrimental effect on the ecological environment.

Please take your waste home with you and, if you are caught short, use a water bottle if you have one. And then take that away with you too.

Remember, there are toilets at the Glen Nevis Visitor Centre so please use them before you start to climb

The paradox of a place like Glen Nevis and the mountain which takes its name is that, as one of

The Ben and Glen Today

Britain's most beautiful wild places, things can get quite busy – especially during the summer months.

Around 200,000 visit the glen every year. Some will climb the mountain but many others will enjoy the many low level walks.

So it is tourism, probably more than anything else, which has brought the biggest changes to the glen.

But the Glen's beauty not only attracts visitors. In the last few years a number of well known films have been shot here including Harry Potter, Braveheart and Rob Roy.

There is an urgent need to make sure this special landscape is protected. That's why organisations such as the Nevis Partnership, Highland Council, John Muir Trust, Foresty Commission, Scottish Natural Heritage and private landowners are working together to make sure this happens.

This is a landscape that has always inspired people. So that it can continue to do so we all need to play a part.

Taking litter and waste away with you, sticking to the proper paths, keeping your dog under control, especially around livestock and ground nesting birds such as ptarmigan. These are small things visitors can do but which make a big difference.

above
Looking up into Coire Leis, with Carn Mor Dearg on the left and Ben Nevis on the right.

Access

Access rules in Scotland are different from those in England and Wales and there is rather more freedom to walk and explore than you might be used to at home.

Thanks to the Land Reform (Scotland) Act of 2003, the general public has the right to be on most land and inland water provided the guidelines set out in the Scottish Outdoor Access Code are followed.

Get to know the code before you go out at www.outdooraccess-scotland.com

When you are in the outdoors the key things to remember are:

Take responsibility for your own actions

Respect the interests of other people

Care for the environment

A Natural Partnership

Caraidean Nibheis

People from all over the world come to visit Ben Nevis and the surrounding landscape. It is, for many, a truly iconic place.

Striking the right balance of protecting this area, whilst at the same time making sure it is accessible and a joy to visit, is one of our biggest challenges.

That's why the Nevis Partnership launched its Friends of Nevis scheme in 2008. It provides a number of different things people can do to support and protect Ben Nevis and the surrounding landscape and help keep it special.

- Make a one-off donation through the Friends of Nevis website (see below for the address) or at one of the collection cairns in the glen.
- Work with us as a volunteer. It's fun and a great way to get outdoors and enjoy the area. There are all sorts of things we need help with, including litter picks, shrub clearance, path-building weekends, wildlife surveys, administration and events.
- Join 'Friends of Nevis'. See below for address.

Visit www.friendsofnevis.co.uk to find out more about volunteering or becoming a friend.

Further information

Tuilleadh Fiosrachaidh

Glen Nevis Visitor Centre

This is a great place to begin your visit. There is a small exhibition on Ben Nevis and the surrounding area, up-to-date weather forecast, books, leaflets, outdoor clothing and snacks. Public toilets are also there – the only ones in the glen.
Open Easter – mid October 8.30am to 5.30pm
Open mid October - Easter 9am to 3pm.
Tel 01392 705922

Scottish Natural Heritage

Scottish Natural Heritage is a Scottish Government body which looks after all of Scotland's nature and landscapes to help people enjoy it, value it and look after it. *www.snh.org.uk*

John Muir Trust

The John Muir Trust is a leading wild land conservation charity, and landowner in Glen Nevis and on Ben Nevis. It helps protect 115,000 hectares of mountain, moorland, rugged coast and wooded glens across Scotland through ownership, partnership and with local communities. *www.jmt.org*

The Forestry Commission

An important landowner around Glen Nevis. It maintains the Braveheart car park and also has a local recreation and communities Forester. Call 01397 702184 or go to *www.forestry.gov.uk/scotland*

Lochaber Mountain Rescue Team

The Lochaber Mountain Rescue team is the busiest in Britain. It was set up in the 1960s and is made up entirely of volunteers. The team is called on when incidents happen that the usual emergency services are unable to get to – such as rescuing a climber stranded on the sheer North Face of Ben Nevis or a canoeist stuck in an inaccessible gorge. *www.lochabermrt.co.uk*
To call them you dial 999 or 112 ask for Police and then Mountain Rescue.

Maps, guides and leaflets

To help you enjoy your visit:
Ordnance Survey Leisure Map No 38 'Ben Nevis and Glencoe' 1:25,000
Ordnance Survey Landranger Map No 41 1:40,000 'Ben Nevis, Fort William and Surrounding Area'
Harvey Maps 'Ben Nevis' Superwalker map 1: 25,000
A special Ben Nevis mini map by Harvey Maps is available from the Glen Nevis Visitor Centre.
A low level walks leaflet published by the Nevis Partnership is available at the Glen Nevis Visitor Centre and outlets in Fort William.
If you want to learn more about wild flowers in the glen the John Muir Trust has published a wild flower leaflet. You can get this from the Glen Nevis Visitor Centre.

Accommodation

If you want to stay in Glen Nevis pop into the Visit Scotland Visitor Information Centre on Fort William High Street. Open all year.
You can also book accommodation through VisitScotland by 'phoning 0845 22 55 121 or go to *www.visitscotland.com*
    The Outdoor Capital of the UK website also lists accommodation in and around Fort William and Glen Nevis. *www.outdoorcapital.co.uk*

Weather forecasts

If you're planning on climbing in the hills make sure you're confident of the weather. For up to date forecasts go to the Glen Nevis Visitor Centre or you can get the very latest forecasts at *www.mwis.org.uk*
If you're walking during the winter months the Scottish Avalanche Information Service (SAIS) has regular updates on avalanche hazards. *www.sais.gov.uk*

Acknowledgement and thanks

Lots of people helped in the creation of this book, sharing generously (and usually for free) their time, photographs, memories, knowledge and experiences.

So a big round of applause to (in no particular order):
- Alex Gillespie for his photographs and inexhaustible patience
- Jimmy Ness for his memories of climbing at Polldubh
- Scottish Natural Heritage, especially Betty Common in the image library
- Alan Kimber www.westcoast-mountainguides.co.uk
- Jennie Robertson for her expertise in ancient history and archaeology
- Ewan Cameron of Glen Nevis House for help with clan history and farming
- Sheila Maclennan for local history
- Hughie and Isie Cameron for social history
- Noel Williams for info. and pics. on geology
- Sarah Lewis of the John Muir Trust for help with flora and fauna in Glen Nevis
- Ian Strachan for sharing his knowledge and pictures of the flora and fauna of the Ben and Glen
- Craig Millar and Picture Library staff of Forestry Commission Scotland
- National Library of Scotland
- Highland Libraries and www.ambaile.org.uk
- Dòmhnall Morris of Comunn na Gàidhlig for translation
- Richard Wallis, Rio Tinto Alcan for help on the background and history of aluminium
- Mike Pescod www.abacusmountaineering.com
- Ian Abernethy for help with local history and images
- Michelle Melville, Highland Council Ranger for input on Gaelic language and culture
- Jim Milligan from the Glen Nevis Visitor Centre
- Bridget Thomas for explaining the wonders of kayaking
- Neil Dalgleish of Hillside Design www.hillsideagency.com
- Joy Biggin for proof-reading

Funding

This book was produced by the Nevis Partnership as part of the Glen Nevis Sense of Place project, which was funded by The European Regional Development Fund, Highland Council, Highlands and Islands Enterprise and the Nevis Partnership.